POLISH CENTRE OF MEDITERRANEAN ARCHAEOLOGY, UNIVERSITY OF WARSAW

Franciszek Pawlicki

The Main Sanctuary of Amun-Re in the Temple of Hatshepsut at Deir el-Bahari

Cover: Hatshepsut offers a pellet of incense to Amun-Re.
An episode of the Daily Ritual depicted in the Statue Room.
Left: The red granite portal leading to the Bark Hall
and to further rooms of the Sanctuary.
(Photo Maciej Jawornicki)

THE STRUCTURE AND ITS RELIGIOUS FUNCTIONS

The temple was called the "Great Mansion of the God of Millions of Years of Amun Djeser-djeseru" thus the Main Sanctuary of Amun-Re might have a splendid form and be of a particular character. The localization and plan of the complex were shaped according to the cult and the ceremonies conducted there. A vast peristyle courtyard is a prelude to the Sanctuary, and its western wall forms an extended façade of the Sanctuary. Its decoration composed of scenes of apotropaic character and rituals of purification with incense and fresh water before Amun indicates the proximity of the Sanctuary. The architecture of the wall with its sequence of low and tall niches, points to the centrally located big entrance to the Sanctuary which leads to one of them (drawing below). This one, housing a statue of the god, being an object of perpetual rituals of the Daily Cult, was located inside the Djeser-djeseru, it means — in the "Holy of the Holiest Place". This localization, which closes the main axis of the temple and being the most western inside the whole terraced building, secures the essential intimacy of the deity. In front of the temple, on an extension of the main axis, a processional way was arranged, and beyond it, on the other side of the Nile, there was the temple complex of Karnak; the festival procession with the bark of Amun-Re started from there to Deir el-Bahari. The spacious Bark Hall, built inside the rock massif, was preceded by a vestibule. Its corbelled vault was protected by a relieving construction composed of huge limestone slabs. Other chapels and niches were cut in the rock. The Sanctuary is a homogenous architectonic construction which is testified by the same arrangement of block levels visible in the walls of its chambers. According to the Egyptian architectural canon, the following chambers are smaller one by one. It is supposed that a temple sanctuary, housing the god, reflects the arrangement of the royal residence: throne hall, royal private room and sleeping room. The Sanctuary in the precinct of Hatshepsut, devoted to Amun-Re and his sacred bark, was a part of the temple devoted to the royal mortuary cult. It focused all the aspects of the royal ideology of Hatshepsut, including her connection with Amun, her divine father. The queen's Osiride statues placed in the four corners of the first chamber protected the holy bark, and her cartouches placed in the tympanums of the side chapels and in the Room of the Statue were protected by the names of Amun-Re. There is enough evidence to assume that Hatshepsut, as a founder of the temple endowed with royal dignity, takes place next to her divine father in the Inner Sanctuary as well.

5
3
2
4
1
6
2 0 2 4 m

Plan of the Sanctuary.

1.Bark Hall;
2. Statue Room;
3-4. Chapels of the Great Ennea
5. Inner Sanctuary (from the 2n
cent. BC – Ptolemaic Sanctuary
6. Ptolemaic Portico.

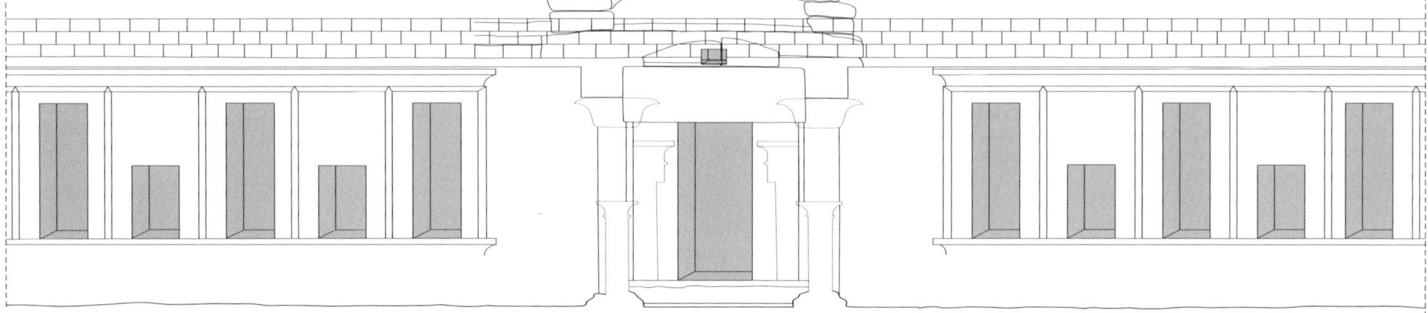

The central part of the West wall of the Upper Courtyard with entrance to the Sanctuary and relieving construction above the Bark Hall in the middle (see also p. 30 and p. 31).
(Opposite) The Sanctuary inside. In the foreground the Statue Room, then the Bark Hall and the Festival Courtyard of the Upper Terrace; view from West to East, in the direction to the temple of Amun-Re in Karnak.

Hatshepsut started to build the Main Sanctuary just after her coronation (c 1473 BC). The features of her representation, her royal titles, and, especially, the presence of the earlier deceased princess Neferure among the living persons, indicate that. Architectonic studies prove that it was one of the earliest finished complexes in the temple. The first modification was conducted during an early stage of building when the façade arrangement and dimensions of the Bark Hall had been changed. The lighting of the cult statue, standing inside the Sanctuary, was changed two times in the reign of Hatshepsut. The replacement of the former limestone gate with the portal made of red Aswan granite was the most spectacular innovation. In the Statue Room, the northern niche, as well as the opposite one, devoted to the Great Theban Ennead under Amun's supervision, was enlarged. The Sanctuary of Amun-Re survived in this form till the end of the New Kingdom functioning as a splendid repository of the holy bark and cult statue. The sculptures and wall decoration were several times destroyed (by Tuthmosis III and Akhenaten) and restored (by Tutankhamun and Horemheb).

In the Third Intermediate Period (1069 – 664 BC), the Sanctuary, as well as other compartments of the Upper Terrace, were used as a cemetery for royal family members, noblemen and Montu priests. For a short time, under Montuemhat – mayor of

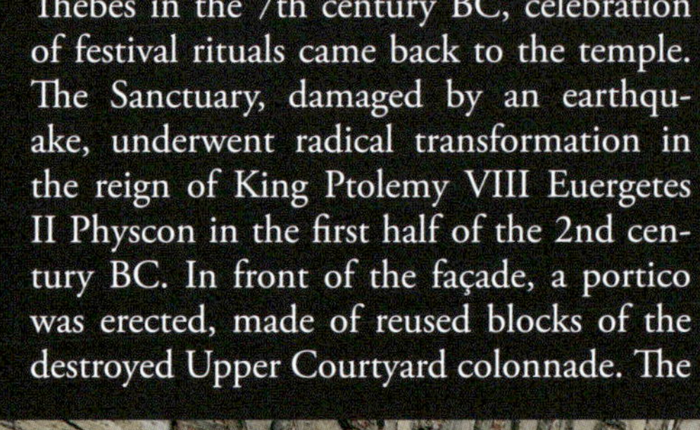

Thebes in the 7th century BC, celebration of festival rituals came back to the temple. The Sanctuary, damaged by an earthquake, underwent radical transformation in the reign of King Ptolemy VIII Euergetes II Physcon in the first half of the 2nd century BC. In front of the façade, a portico was erected, made of reused blocks of the destroyed Upper Courtyard colonnade. The

niches and skylights in the Bark Hall were blocked. The last room of the Sanctuary, then housing the cult statue of Amun-Re, was rearranged and transformed into the cult chapel of the deified Amenhotep-son-of-Hapu and Imhotep. Graffiti on the walls and discovered archaeological finds indicate that the Sanctuary was also visited in Roman times. In Byzantine times, the chapel was included into the monastery of Saint Phoibammon which flourished on the Upper Terrace since the end of the 6th century AD.

(Above) The corbelled vault hollowed out underneath to achieve a vaulted effect i the Bark Hall. The painted blue ceiling is covered with a layer of soot and, as th result of high temperature, the yellow painted stars changed their colour to red; thes are remains of activity in Byzantine times.

(Far left and centre) The Southern Chapel of the Great Theban Ennead, the Room o Cult Statue and former Inner Sanctuary. In the Ptolemaic period, in this last room all the original limestone blocks were removed and replaced with sandstone ones.

AMUN-RE – THE LORD OF THE SANCTUARY

In the New Kingdom, Amun, closely identified with the sun god Re, became the most popular and widely venerated deity. It was believed that, as a manifestation of the universal solar god he creates, sustains and regenerates life. After absorbing the attributes of the ancient Theban war god Montu, he personified the military power of the Egyptian Kingdom. His absolute supremacy in the Sanctuary is best illustrated by the decoration of the granite lintel portal above the entrance. The enthroned god takes on the form of two twin statues with their backs to one another with figures of kneeling kings set up in front of them. Scenes of the same nature and similar compositions adorn the tympanums of the eastern and western walls of the Bark Hall. As the host of the Sanctuary, he welcomes the entering Hatshepsut and impressive images of his sacred bark gracing the walls of the first shrine. It is his statue which is worshipped in scenes decorating the rear walls of the six niches in the Bark Hall, in the Statue Room and finally in the Inner Sanctuary itself.

It is of significance that there is no ityphallic image of Amun in the Sanctuary rooms, even though that is the shape that the god's processional statue took. He is depicted in his classic stance, enthroned or standing with a *was* scepter (symbol of power) in his hand, extended towards the king. The god's titles distinguish between particular almost identical gods' images. The variety of epithets was surely meant to bring to mind all his different features and functions. Significantly, the Ancient Egyptians themselves called him "Amun is rich in names". Alongside the traditional ones, the most prestigious and eminent titles as "King of the Gods", "Lord of the Thrones of Both Lands", "Ruler of Thebes" or "Lord of Heaven", several times he is endowed with epithets emphasizing his constant presence at Deir el-Bahari as "Foremost of Djeser-djeseru". However, no evidence of his stone cult statue was found in the Sanctuary.

The figure of enthroned Amun-Re restored in the post-Amarna period. His head is adorned with a flat-topped cap pulled down on the temples, the characteristic high crown composed of two ostrich feathers mounted on it. A wide necklace decorates the chest and there are bracelets on the arms and legs as well as a beard ceremonially curled at the end. The kilt is yellow, whereas the jacket is decorated with a characteristic feather ornament. The tympanum of the West wall of the Bark Hall.

(From left) The statue of the king holding a fan in front of the naos of Amun-Re on the southern wall of the Bark Hall. The god is endowed with the title "King of the Gods". In the middle, the face of Amun-Re carved in the Statue Room carefully restored in the post-Amarna period. Beside, the recut name of the deity and his epithet "Lord of the Thrones of Both Lands" is visibly lower than the original inscription enumerating offerings to Amun-Re. North wall of the vestibule of the Sanctuary.

(Left) The estate of Amun. Garden divided by mud-brick walls into numerous identical plots with planted long-leaf lettuce consecrated to the god. During the reign of Hatshepsut, the domain of Amun was supervised by the steward Senenmut, a well known government official. (Right) In the Sanctuary, the depiction of the estate neighbours the chaotic regions symbolized by a papyrus marsh with waterfowl and a pond with fish. Reliefs depicted at the bottommost register of the South wall of the Bark Hall.

THE FEAST OF THE VALLEY

Richly decorated ram-headed aegis of Amun fastened to the stern of his sacred processional bark. The ends of gods' barks or boats were traditionally decorated with a shield-like aegis surmounted with a deity's image. Amun's aegis was the only image of the god seen by the crowds during his festive peregrination from Karnak to Deir el-Bahari. Thus it was the god's personification acting during his festival procession. The sacred creature in the form of the ram with extremely curved horns most probably suggested the procreative limitless energy of the god hidden in the shrine. The god wears a multicolored atef crown ornamented with horns, uraei and a solar disk. At the bottom there is partly preserved semicircular wide necklace wsh, a favorite ornament of gods and kings. Doubtless, a shield-like ram-headed aegis had a protective and regenerative functions as well. The latter is pointed out by an image of scarab associated with the concepts of eternal renewal depicted in the aegis' center. Relief carved on the North wall of the Bark Hall.

The origins of the annual festival known in the New Kingdom as the Beautiful Feast of the Valley date back to the Middle Kingdom. The feast linked with the god Amun-Re is evidenced for the first time in the temple at Deir al-Bahari constructed by the ruler of 11 Dynasty, king Nebhepetre Mentuhotep II, where the joint cult of the god and the king was celebrated. It seems that the feast celebrated during the second month of Shemu (summer season) referred to the popular rituals associated with the goddess Hathor, a patroness of cemeteries traditionally situated in Western Thebes. Its first depictions on the walls of the temples of Karnak (Red Chapel) and Deir el-Bahari are dated to the reign of queen Hatshepsut. The festival led by the queen and her co-regent Tuthmosis III, noblemen and priests carrying the sacred bark of Amun-Re, involved a river journey across the Nile and a land procession to the royal temples on the west bank. The sacred bark was accompanied by musicians and dancers, courtiers and priests carrying divine standards and liturgical equipment, offerings and portable statues of the royal family members. Troops of soldiers armed with shields, axes and spears ensured the security of the sacred bark itself, as well as of the rulers and royal dignitaries. Behind the river part of the journey with royal ships was towed the huge boat Userhat with the sacred bark of Amun-Re and a flotilla of smaller boats. The festival march was continued on the west bank. Offerings and purification rituals were made in the Lower Temple built on the outskirts of the desert and in the Station for the Bark constructed halfway to the procession's final destination. The procession walked along the causeway towards the temple of Hatshepsut at Deir el-Bahari. Its main Sanctuary was already prepared to accommodate the statue of the god and his sacred bark. Here, in the first chamber the final rituals of the festival were carried out before the bark and the god spent the night. In the morning more offering rituals were performed and the procession with sacred bark turned back to the Karnak temple. With time, the feast became more elaborate. The barks of the goddess Mut and god Khonsu joined the procession, which visited the royal mortuary temples built in Western Thebes.

(Top left)
During the Feast of the Valley, Amun left his temple in Karnak, crossed the Nile and taken to Deir el-Bahari. When travelling, the divine image was placed in a small shrine (k3r) set upon a processional bark. The god's image could be hidden from view by a richly decorated veil visible in the lower part of the shrine. The gilded wooden shrine has the typical rectangular form with a pitched roof curved to the front. At the top, the naos is adorned with a frieze of alternately depicted falcons and cobras embellished with sun-disks. Beneath, there was a large depiction of a vulture with outstretched wings and a uraeus frieze. In the middle, large-scale hieroglyphs forming the name of Horemheb were protected by two winged goddesses Maat. At the bottom, the frieze was additionally embellished with the cartouches of Horemheb. North wall of the Bark Hall.

(Below left and right)
The procession of four statues of fecundity deities in two rows holding torches. They appear in the form of the Nile gods with sagging breasts and swollen bellies with a bunch of lotus flowers on top of their heads. Behind them there are two containers with ten torches in each receptacle. In front of divinities procession there was an image of Hatshepsut erased under Tuthmosis III along with the sign sema-tawy (entwined lotus and papyrus, the plants of Upper and Lower Egypt) meaning unity and enduringness of queen's dominion carved below Hatshepsut's figure. Torches were kindled and set round the bark until the dawn of each day during the visit of the sacred bark in the Sanctuary. Its support was surrounded by four basins filled with milk which presumably helped to represent the sacred harbour of the bark. Torches were extinguished in the milk and the festive procession of the god moved back to the Karnak temple.

THE SACRED BARK OF AMUN-RE

Throughout the New Kingdom, the overall shape of the ceremonial bark of Amun-Re remained unchanged. From the beginning a wooden boat, which was a miniature of a river transport barge was always decorated with prow and stern images of the heads of a ram — the sacred animal of Amun. A richly decorated and gilded naos for the cult statue of the god was placed on board in the middle of the hull. For the occasion of the festival, the statue was especially adorned with jewellery. The portable bark was equipped with a low sledge-shaped stretcher and long poles carried over the shoulders of priests during the festival procession from Karnak to Deir el-Bahari.

In the Sanctuary, the bark was set on a stone pedestal in the middle of the shrine as was shown on the reliefs. During the reign of Hatshepsut, the bark was supported by three wooden bars each held by six priests. Not a single processional bark of Amun-Re has been found but it is calculated that its total length with carrying poles measured four and a half metres. At least from the end of the Eighteenth Dynasty the bark was enlarged. Because of that in the Ramesside period the number of poles increased to five carried on shoulders of thirty priests. As the barks widened to accommodate more priests as carriers, some gates at the temples needed to be enlarged.

During the Amarna period, the agents of Akhenaten studiously removed from the walls of the Sanctuary all figures of the gods along with images of the sacred bark of Amun-Re. The restorations of the barks depictions started already in the reign of Tutankhamun and were later on reworked and usurped by Horemheb. At this time, the entire composition of the bark was significantly increased at the expense of the previous decoration. Imposing *atef* crowns topped by a solar disk were added to the heads of the rams. The roof of the shrine was decorated with a frieze containing a cryptographic inscription of the name of Horemheb. On the starboard traditionally were present goddesses Maat and Hathor and the royal banners with figures of sphinxes.

(Top) Painted in blue and yellow head of the ram on the prow of the processional bark renovated by Horemheb. (Centre) A shield-like aegis richly decorated with floral motifs. In the middle of the disk there is a depiction of a winged scarab associated with the generative forces of the rising sun. Above the scarab there is a flower of lotus and two pendulous royal cobras. (Bottom) Images of Horemheb on the boat deck and a frieze composed of cobras, falcons and the king's name Djeserkheperure painted on the veil of the naos. Above the frieze there is a kneeling figure of Heh - the god of infinity.

A drawing and a photo of the sacred bark inside the Sanctuary at Deir el-Bahari during the Feast of the Valley. The bark with the naos for the god's statue in the centre equipped with a sledge resting on a pedestal. The relief was renovated in the time of Horemheb. His name protected by two figures of winged goddesses Maat (see one of them above left) is visible in the naos centre in form of the falcon of Horus („Hr") standing on the hieroglyphic signs "m" and "heb". Beneath the naos there is a partly preserved group of kneeling figures symbolizing the souls of Pe and Nekhen worshiping Amun and his sacred bark. Some other episodes of this festival are depicted on the East and on the North walls of the Upper Courtyard.

FEASTS AND RITUALS

The Main Sanctuary of Amun-Re was a temporary shrine for his sacred bark and statue during the annual journey of the god from Karnak to the Valley of Deir el-Bahari on the west bank. Here the processional bark stood in an elongated rectangular Bark Hall. Its impressive depictions with piles of offerings are presented on both the longitudinal walls of the chamber. The offerings before the bark are made by the living members of the royal family: Hatshepsut, Tuthmosis III and princess Neferure. The deceased ancestors Tuthmosis I, Ahmes, Tuthmosis II and princess Neferubity (Hatshepsut's sister who died in childhood) participated in the celebration in the western part of the room. The all-night ceremonies ended at dawn, when torches were extinguished in four pools of milk.

The festival procession with the sacred bark arrived in Deir el-Bahari once a year. However, other feasts and a series of cultic rituals were performed for the statue of the god Amun by temple priests each day. The Daily Ritual was a fundamental part of the cultic ritual celebrated in the Sanctuary where the image of the god dwelt on a permanent basis; its proper performance assured favour from the god. Selected episodes of the Daily Ritual were represented in the niches of the Bark Hall and on the walls of the Statue Room. The choice of rituals focused on purification rites with water, incense and pellets of natron. They illustrated the liturgy of animating the divine statue. This liturgy was also celebrated in front of the statues of Hatshepsut in the form of the god Osiris standing in every corner of the Bark Hall. The queen and the other members of her family were the beneficiaries of yet one more liturgy. Reliefs on the lateral walls of the niches depicted Hatshepsut and the other members of the royal family sitting on a throne before an offering table. The shortened version of the offering list carved above the offering table ensured prosperity and abundant food for the kings after death. It demonstrates that the Sanctuary was a cultic place not only for Amun-Re but also for the king.

The Daily Ritual. Queen Hatshepsut pouring water over the god's statue. The ritual was connected with the ceremony of revivification of the cult statue. The Statue Room.

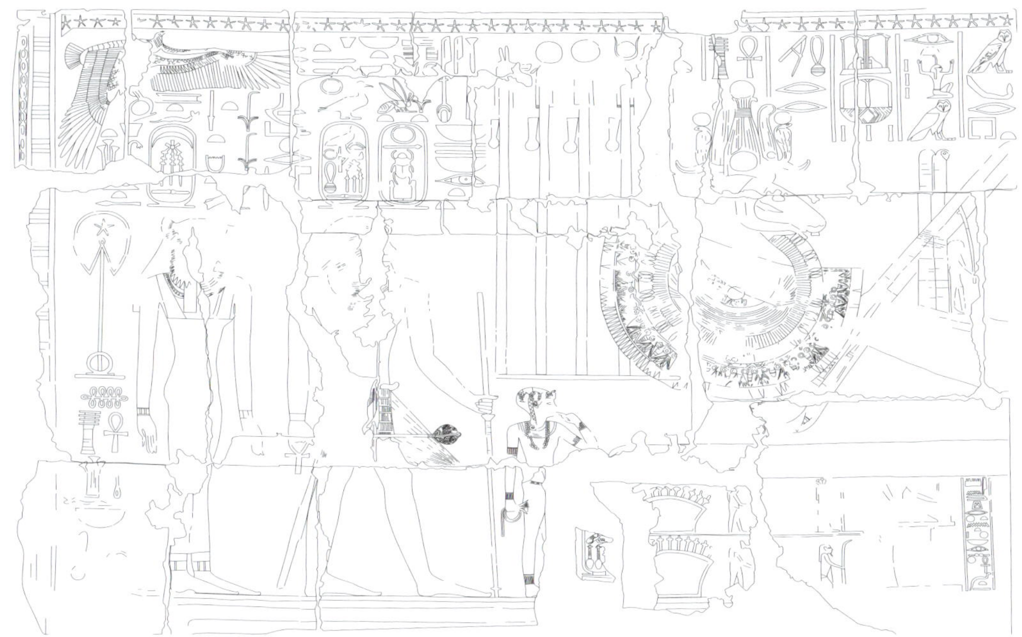

Deceased members of the royal family during the offering ritual before the sacred bark. North wall of the Bark Hall.

Tuthmosis III kneeling with white bread. Relief from the East wall of the Bark Hall.

Five pellets of Upper and five pellets of Lower Egyptian natron offered by Tuthmosis III to Amun-Re. North wall of the Statue Room.

Hatshepsut behind an offering table addressed by the Junmutef-priest. Drawing of the decoration of the side wall of the niche in the Bark Hall.

OFFERINGS FOR GOD AND KING

The offerings given to Amun-Re, in front of his sacred bark, were depicted not only in their classic figural form, laying on tables full of goods and on reed mats, but they were also represented in the form of lists. Above the bark, in two rows, there are 40 registers which form the temple offering list of type "D" bearing names of products, their graphic representations and their quantities. The lists are identical on both the Bark Hall walls. Most of the goods described or depicted in painted relief are traditional offerings given in the Offering Table Ritual. There are breads and cakes of different shape, vegetables (salad, cucumber, onion, garlic, and and leek), fruits (including dates, grapes, and pomegranates), poultry (geese, ducks), parts of roast and a haunch. There is a rich representation of drinks: different kinds of beer and wine, honey and fresh water, they were brought in pots, vases and jars. Features of the decoration of some of the vessels imitated stone vessels, others — painted yellow – symbolised vessels made of gold. The quantities of lettuce and bouquets of flowers, here open calyxes and buds of lotus — traditionally regarded as a symbol of life and resurrection, are of special notice; it was believed that the lotus was filled with the smell of god. Occasionally, to the standard list of offerings, the name of a tool was added, for example the name of the knife essential to prepare an animal offering during a festival ceremony, or a censer, or precious cosmetic pigments and oils used in the ceremony of caring for a cult statue.

In each of the niches of the Bark Hall, offerings, however in lesser quantity, are also represented on their side walls, where the Ritual of the Offering Table is represented. Here also, the figural representation is accompanied by an offering table list which this time consists of 22 names. The quantity of offerings, presented to the ruler seated in front of the offering table, reaches thousands of pieces. A special offering formula guaranties such a quantity of offerings, wherein a thousand of bread, a thousand of beer, a thousand of olives, a thousand of oxen and poultry are enumerated (see drawing at the bottom of p. 15).

(Above) A magnificent heap of offerings presented in front of the sacred bark of Amun-Re, depicted on the North wall of the Bark Hall.
(Below) A censer handle in the form of Horus' head depicted on the South wall of the Bark Hall.

(Left) An offering list depicted above a variety of offerings on the North wall of the Bark Hall.
(Below) Two vessels bearing clear traces of Hatshepsut's name in cartouches, painted black. Her other names, painted on vessels (bottom left) before the sacred bark, have been removed after her death.

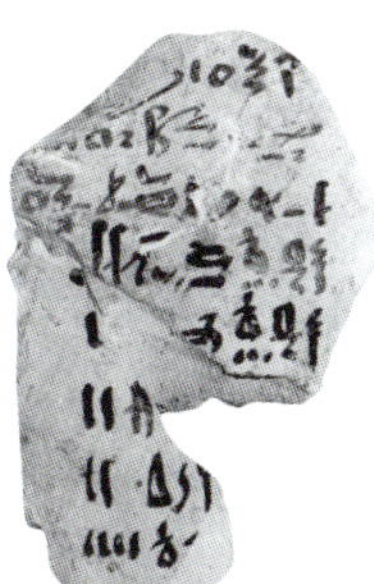

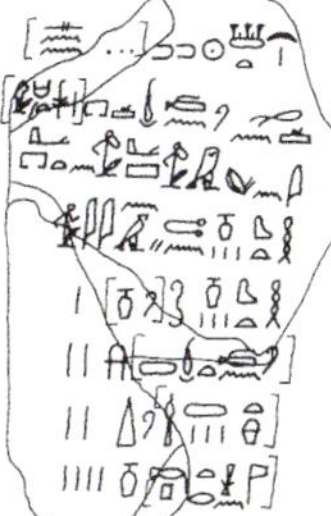

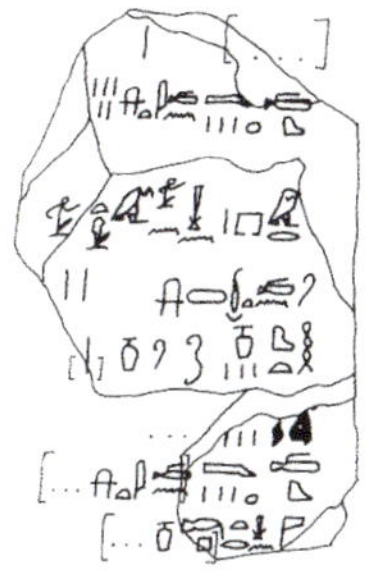

Fragmentary hieratic ostrakon found during the protective work undertaken by the Polish-Egyptian Mission above the Sanctuary of Amun-Re. Presumably the ostrakon was thrown into the triangular chamber above the Bark Hall at the time when the relieving stone structure was still under construction. The text comprises two lists of offerings brought by two officials: Senenmut and Tjennay to the temple of Hatshepsut at Deir el-Bahari on an unknown occasion. Among enumerating goods there are sacks of white and wdn.t-bread, jars of Nubian beer, baskets of fruits and of incense for fumigation. The latter item was delivered in pots destined to be burnt during religious ceremonies. One can notice the difference between the formal enumeration of the offerings presented on the walls of the Bark Hall and scribal record of items to be prepared for cultic performance of some specific nature.

THE ROYAL FAMILY

The portrait of Hatshepsut in white khat headdress. The uraeus serpent at the queen's brow with the undulating tail over the top of the head protects Hatshepsut against evil. There is no evidence of a chin strap attached to the false beard; however the beard itself is preserved. In spite of the masculine dress, the portrait has distinctive feminine features. The most conspicuous are long cosmetic lines of the almond-shaped wide eye, small mouth and rounded chin. The corner of the quite full mouth is raised in a slight smile and emphasized by circular hole. However, most surprising is the pinkish or light-red hue of the queen's skin in contrast to the traditional iconography of female flesh in a yellow hue. Detail of the relief depicting Hatshepsut offering a ball of incense to the statue of Amun-Re (see cover photo). South wall of the Statue Room.

The Bark Hall in the Sanctuary of Amun-Re is the only place in the Deir el-Bahari temple, where all members of Hatshepsut's family are depicted; both the living and the dead persons. The latter including queen's parents Tuthmosis I and queen Ahmes, her stepbrother and husband Tuthmosis II and princess Neferubity, a sister of Hatshepsut, are gathered in the western section of the shrine. The world of the living represented by Hatshepsut herself, her stepson Tuthmosis III and queen's daughter princess Neferure is shown in the eastern part of the hall. These two separate worlds meet together around the sacred bark and in the six niches of the Bark Hall. It is queen Hatshepsut who forms the bridge appearing in each one of them accompanying alternately Tuthmosis I, Ahmes or Tuthmosis II, and by her co-ruler Tuthmosis III. Obviously the depictions of the queen's ancestors would emphasize her royal descent and played an important role in the legitimacy of her rights to the royal throne. Thus it is not a coincidence that in the middle niches located in the vicinity of the sacred bark of Amun-Re, Hatshepsut is shown in the company of her father. Apparently the queen used all possibilities to present herself as the heiress of her father Tuthmosis I. She adopted the full titular of a pharaoh including the throne name Maatkare written down in royal cartouche.

Among the living could not be missed the depictions of Tuthmosis III who together with Hatshepsut presents offerings to the sacred bark and celebrates the Daily Ritual before Amun-Re in the Statue Room. Despite his activity, the dominant position of Hatshepsut as the foremost officiant is evident. She is shown wearing the ceremonial attire of the Egyptian king however, in spite of the masculine dress, her figures have a clearly feminine aspect. Depending on the ritual (or the location of the scene) she appears in different headdress and crowns. There is no sufficient evidence to establish in full the design of the royal statuary in the Sanctuary suite. Nevertheless four "Osiride" statues of Hatshepsut show that at least in the Bark Hall queen's position was not confined to the role of an officiant.

The almost perfectly preserved image of king Tuthmosis I carved on the side-wall of the central niche of the Bark Hall opposite the figure of his daughter queen Hatshepsut. Two middle niches blocked in the Ptolemaic period were discovered and reopened only in 1981 by the Polish–Egyptian Mission. The king is sitting before the offering-table and before list of offerings presented above in tabular form. He wears a nemes headdress painted in yellow with uraeus at the brow. Originally the head-cloth was striped but today only traces of pleats marked in red are visible. Much more of blue pigment is preserved on the king's false beard as well on his broad necklace. His pleated kilt is yellow. The stylistic similarities (i.e. a straight nose, slightly intriguing smile, almond-shaped eye) between this image and the reliefs of Tuthmosis II and Tuthmosis III are quite obvious. The royal throne is painted in a sequence of blue and red strips. At the bottom of each side of the throne there was a sema-tawy motif symbolizing the union of Upper and Lower Egypt. Today heraldic plants (lily and papyrus) knotted around the hieroglyphic sign for union are barely visible. Central niche located in the North wall of the Bark Hall.

The original portrait of king Tuthmosis II, late husband of Hatshepsut, and the father of Tuthmosis III. The relief has sustained considerable damage. The forehead, nose and corner of the eye are missing. In spite of this, the king's face retains its Tuthmoside distinguishing character and great deal of expression. His almond-shaped eye descends slightly down and a slightly intriguing smile enlivens the face. The ruler wears a red bowl shaped crown desheret traditionally associated with Lower Egypt. The red polychrome of the crown and blue colour of false beard are unpreserved while remains of polychrome are still visible on the broad necklace. The king's face is painted in a deep red colour. The exposed ear is carefully developed. Detail of the relief carved in the bottommost register of the North wall of the Bark Hall.

A somewhat idealized portrait of Tuthmosis III in pleated nemes headdress with a uraeus-serpent at the brow. The image of the young king, Hatshepsut's nephew and stepson, is full of charm. Apparently the style of the portrait was based on a general Tuthmoside family likeness. However in comparison with the image of Hatshepsut, the king's eye is clearly narrower and the line of his eyebrow painted in blue is less curved. The false beard attached to the small rounded chin is painted in blue as well. This colour was traditionally associated with deities. The clarity of outlines and juxtaposition of the blue against red colour of the skin and yellow of the headdress results in an exceptionally vivid impression of portrait. Detail of the representation of Tuthmosis III offering spherical nw-jars to Amun-Re on the Bark Hall's West wall.

The portrait of queen Ahmes, wife of Tuthmosis I and mother of queen Hatshepsut carved on the South wall of the Bark Hall. Despite numerous and prestigious titles as Hereditary Princess, Lady of all Women and Mistress of the Two Lands, little is known about her predecessors and royal family relations. It is puzzling that she was never called a King's Daughter. However she was endowed with one of the most important and hereditary titles "God's Wife of Amun". In this role she participated in the temple ceremonies and rituals. In the Main Sanctuary of Amun-Re, queen Ahmes, as a princess of royal blood, wears headdress of Egyptian queens topped with a protective uraeus at the brow. Vulture wings spread round her head in the act of protection. She is titled King's Sister and Great Royal Wife. Apart from her two almost identical depictions on the walls of the Bark Hall she was also presented in the western niche of the first chamber sitting before the offering-table while her daughter Hatshepsut was depicted on the opposite wall of the same niche. Drawing after a photo of stone from the collection in Norwich Museum.

Princess Neferubity, Hatshepsut's prematurely dead sister. It is supposed that the daughter of Tuthmosis I and queen Ahmes died in childhood. She is conventionally depicted as a naked girl in the traditional pose of a child holding a thumb to her mouth and with lotus flower in the other hand. Her cranium is conventionally elongated with the sidelock of youth and uraeus at the brow. Although naked she is richly adorned with bracelets on hands and legs, a string of beads and necklace on the breast and with a flower worn in her hair. An artist's reconstruction and drawing of the relief carved on the North wall of the Bark Hall.

Princess Neferure, the only child of Hatshepsut and Tuthmosis II. Little is known of her life and career at the royal court. Following the death of her father, she appears in public alongside Hatshepsut and Tuthmosis III. Although she was often titled God's Wife, the religious office traditionally assumed by the royal daughters at that time, the figures of the God's Wife in the Red Chapel built by Hatshepsut in Karnak were left anonymous, most probably because of Neferure's premature death. In the Sanctuary she took part alongside her mother and Tuthmosis III in the offering ceremony before the sacred bark of Amun-Re. Here depicted as an adult person dressed in white robe with the characteristic attributes of the princess: scepter hts, a ritual object associated with the act of consecration, mace and ankh. The head of the princess is decorated with a calathos, diadem and uraeus. Relief carved on the North wall of the Bark Hall.

ICONOGRAPHY: DAMAGING AND RENOVATION

The walls of the temple are covered with depictions of the celebration of the Amun-Re Holy Bark festival and the rituals of the Daily Cult taking place around the statue of the deity. This relief cycle remained undestroyed from Hatshepsut's time till the Ptolemaic period. During that period, some changes and modifications happened, of course. Some of reliefs were hacked off, others renovated or replaced by a new one. The first changes were ordered already by Hatshepsut herself. The reliefs in the Statue Room were repainted and the North Chapel was restructured. Major changes in wall decoration and in whole Sanctuary were made at the end of the reign of Tuthmosis III. The names and representations of Hatshepsut, who was the founder of the temple, were hacked off (below, on the left side of the photo). What is interesting, not all references were removed. All queen's reliefs and small cartouches on offering pots in the vestibule and in the Bark Hall were meticulously destroyed. However, other Hatshepsut representation in less fine rooms remained untouched. This may indicate that after her death the cult activity took place mainly in this first hall. Later, king Akhenaten ordered to remove all images of Amun, his names and titles and also the reliefs of other gods in both chapels of the Ennead. All these decorations were renovated in their original form in the reign of Horemheb (below, on the right side of the photo). The biggest changes are visible in reliefs concerning the sacred bark. They were renovated two times: by Tutankhamun, and later by Horemheb which we know thanks to the cartouches of the latter. The final picture of the sacred bark was much bigger than the original one therefore some of the decoration above and beneath it was removed.

The image of princess Neferure situated on southern side of the jamb of a granite portal leading to the Sanctuary. Hatshepsut ordered its replacement by the figure of queen Ahmes. The face of the princess with small straight nose and gently drawn chin remained unchanged. However the original wig of Neferure was swapped for the royal vulture crown – the attribute of queen. The scepter hts that Neferure had held originally was scratched out and the mace was removed. The name of the princess was changed to the name of Ahmes and her title "God's Wife" (hemet-netjer) was removed. The reason behind this change might be the death of Neferure at a young age. As a consequence Hatshepsut put much effort to honor her parents Ahmes and Tuthmosis I.

A fragment of inscription from the passage between the Bark Hall and the Statue Room. Hatshepsut's name was destroyed according to the order of Tuthmosis III. Only the sun disk remained of the queen's name. Later on, Amun's name was removed by Akhenaten and restored after the Amarna period. The name Djeser-akhet remained unchanged.

Drawing of the decoration carved on the northern wall of the niche in the Bark Hall. The original picture of Hatshepsut (red colour) presenting a vessel with pellets of incense was replaced by representation of Tuthmosis III with two globular nw vessels for water or wine in the scene of celebration of the Daily Ritual before Amun-Re. However, the inscription describing this episode of the ritual remained unchanged and still refers to offering pellets of incense. On the other hand, Amun's epithets were changed and his title "Residing in Djeser-djeseru" was abandoned.

AMUN-RE AND THE GREAT ENNEAD

View of the inside of the northern transverse chapel dedicated to the divinities of the Great Theban Ennead. The tympanum of its rear wall is decorated with the enthroned figures of Amun and Atum in antithetic position. In the lower register the latter is accompanied by Theban god Montu.

In the temple at Deir el-Bahari the gods of the Great Theban Ennead are present only during exceptionally important feasts or events. Such as the announcement of the divine birth of Hatshepsut depicted in the Northern Middle Portico, queen's coronation represented in the vestibule of the Shrine of the goddess Hathor or confirmation her rights to the throne of Egypt shown in the Upper Portico on the Third Terrace. Obviously, the offering ceremonies celebrated before the sacred bark were important enough to justify their presence in the Main Sanctuary. Furthermore, the Great Ennead had no temple of its own in Thebes, while their essence as a hypostasis of Amun, presenting all the aspects of the God-Creator predestined them to be present and be worshipped in his Sanctuary. Amun was omnipotent, present everywhere combined and separated at the same time from the Theban Ennead. More so, his eminent title of "King of the Gods" referred to his specific relation with the Theban Ennead headed by Montu and composed of fifteen deities. In the New Kingdom, Amun had gradually absorbed the attributes of Montu and became the most important and widely venerated divinity in Thebes.

Figures of the college of the Great Theban Ennead appeared as the addressee of an offering ritual on the walls of both southern and northern transverse chapels of the complex. The assembly composed of the Heliopolitan and Theban deities is presided over by Atum and Montu, shown enthroned on the rear walls of the two transverse rooms. The joint presence of Amun and Atum on the tympanum of the northern chapel illustrates that despite the progressing assimilation of the Theban deity with the Heliopolitan counterpart, the two remained distinct deities and Atum continued to be venerated. The longer walls of both chapels are filled with representations of a college of gods. Divinities with Heliopolitan roots were gathered together in the Northern Chapel, while those associated with the region of Thebes were brought together in the opposite one. The only exception is Atum and Montu depicted in both chapels. All gods were of mummiform shape, sitting in a row on thrones and holding the *was* scepter and the *ankh* symbol. The epithets bestowed on them emphasized their presence in the Sanctuary of Amun-Re at Deir el-Bahari.

(Left) The enthroned mummiform deities of the college of the Great Ennead. The leftmost goddess Tjenenet is closely associated with the Theban god Montu with a symbol of the uterus on her head. Before her there is the figure of the goddess Hathor with the solar disk between the cow's horns. Both deities depicted on the western wall of the south transversal chapel. The depictions were destroyed under Akhenaten and recarved in a post-Amarna period in plaster which has been partly flaked away.
(Beside) The figures of the goddess Isis titled "Foremost of Djeser-djeseru" and almost completely destroyed representation of the chthonic god Osiris. Only the back of the figure and of the throne is preserved as well as the text above. Osiris like other deities of the Heliopolitan roots is endowed with the epithet "Residing in Djeser-djeseru". Relief carved on the east wall of the north transverse chapel.

Tuthmosis III with a pile of divine offerings in the presence of two deities of the Ennead and emblem of the royal ka. The king dressed in the nemes headcloth and short kilt held the staff and mace typical features of this sacrificing ritual. Before a pile of offerings there are two mummiform figures: a companion of Montu goddess Junit titled "daughter of Re" and "Lady of Heaven" and the Heliopolitan god Atum. Both seated on thrones with symbols of power and life. Surprisingly queen Hatshepsut is included among the assembly of the Ennead. The emblem of her royal ka along with the Horus name is presented directly behind the deities. They took upon themselves the role of an assembly of the queen's divine ancestors, sanctifying her right to ascend to the throne of Upper and Lower Egypt. The enthroned figures of divinities were destroyed by the agents of Akhenaten and recarved in the post-Amarna period. The name of Hatshepsut was left intact as originally carved. Relief from the eastern wall of the south transverse chapel.

RESEARCH AND DISCOVERIES

Years of research of the Polish-Egyptian Archeological and Restoration Mission have brought more and more information about changes in the Sanctuary and its function. Egyptological research and discoveries made during restoration have allowed, among others, the reconstruction of the building history and appearance of the last room of the Sanctuary complex – the Inner Sanctuary. For a long period it was believed that this chapel was carved in the rock in the reign of Ptolemy VIII Euergetes II Physcon (170-116 BC) only. It appeared, with no doubts, that this chapel was designed and made in Hatshepsut's reign. This is testified by the newly discovered original blocks with the queen's representation. In the Inner Sanctuary, a statue was located and daily rituals were celebrated round it. The discovery of two middle niches in the Bark Hall was not less important to determine the final architectural form of the Sanctuary's first room. It also helped to reconstruct the full cycle of rituals of the Daily Cult and the Offering Ritual, celebrated here. The fragments of blocks, that were used in the Ptolemaic period to fill the niches, allowed the reconstruction of the wall decoration below the representation of the holy bark of Amun-Re. The fragments were used to reconstruct the *sema-tawy* scene which indicates the exceptional role of the bark – the symbol of the union of the Two Lands (of Upper and Lower Egypt) and of the god himself as well.

Above the Bark Hall, during the work to protect the ceiling slabs, hieratic graffiti and ostraca were found. They essentially contributed to the knowledge of history of the Sanctuary building. This new epigraphic material allows the determination of the chronology of phases of the Sanctuary building, to specify the type of offerings, and extend the list of persons involved in building and decoration of the complex. The inscriptions (Demotic and Greek), found in one of the mentioned above niches in the Bark Hall, contain names of persons who visited the Sanctuary in the early Ptolemaic period. Some of the finds relate to the period when the Sanctuary did not act in its primary cult function. These are coins, left by visitors, dated to the reign of Constantine the Great and his sons (AD 4th cent.) discovered in the Bark Hall. The purpose of visit is of no importance (perhaps it was pagan cult religious visit). The discoveries testify to the condition of the building which, after almost two thousand years after Hatshepsut's reign, was still accessible.

Opening of the middle niche in the South wall of the Bark Hall, the niche was closed in Ptolemaic period.

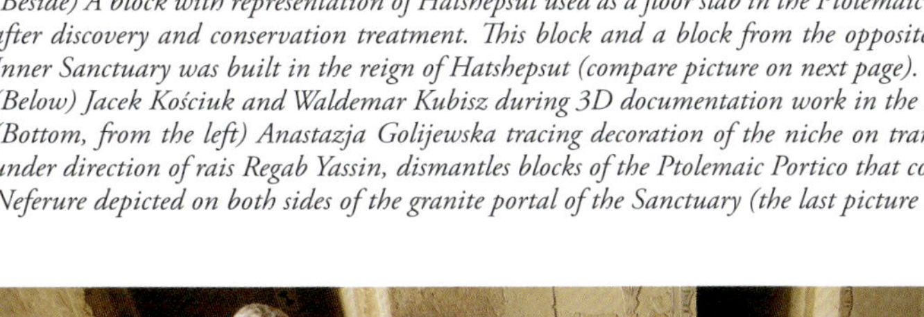

(Beside) A block with representation of Hatshepsut used as a floor slab in the Ptolemaic Sanctuary, its condition after discovery and conservation treatment. This block and a block from the opposite jamb confirm that the Inner Sanctuary was built in the reign of Hatshepsut (compare picture on next page).
(Below) Jacek Kościuk and Waldemar Kubisz during 3D documentation work in the Bark Hall.
(Bottom, from the left) Anastazja Golijewska tracing decoration of the niche on transparent film; the team, under direction of rais Regab Yassin, dismantles blocks of the Ptolemaic Portico that covered figures of princess Neferure depicted on both sides of the granite portal of the Sanctuary (the last picture to the right).

CULT STATUE ILLUMINATION

Throughout the history of Egyptian architecture, the skylights for illumination were usually placed directly below the junction of the roof and the wall or in the ceiling of the flat roofed shrine. In the Sanctuary of Amun-Re partly cut in the rock massif, the way to illuminate the cult statue led through the special system of skylights located in the walls of the Bark Hall and the Statue Room. This arrangement deserves special attention. Although very similar forms of the skylights to those set in the Sanctuary are already known from the architecture of the Old and the Middle Kingdom, in the temple of Hatshepsut an architect had to calculate and calibrate the dimensions and geometry two of them and correlate their arrangement with the astronomical orientation of the temple. The alignment of the Sanctuary oriented towards the sun on the East – West axis of the solar journey was clearly made to permit a precisely controlled influx of sunlight penetrating through the light boxes locating in the walls of the Bark Hall. The section of the external skylight placed in the outer wall is much bigger than the internal one located in the western wall of the Bark Hall. The mouth of the latter is formed almost in the shape of a narrowed slit. It is certain that both skylights were arranged prior to the construction of the walls of the Bark Hall.

Twice a year a statue of Amun kept in the innermost chamber of the Sanctuary was illuminated by the rising sun. A luminous flux was precisely directed through the narrow aperture of the inner skylight. According to the onsite astronomical measurements and having regard to the changes in the inclination of the ecliptic to the celestial equator, it was calculated that during the reign of queen Hatshepsut, such a phenomenon lasting about ten days occurred in mid-November and in the middle of February. These dates were determined by the winter time and the weakened activity of the sun. The illumination by sunrays of the face of the statue of Amun-Re could symbolize the rebirth and the revitalization of the sun god. This was of particular significance since the Sanctuary was situated beneath the Theban massif considered as the symbolic site of the setting sun.

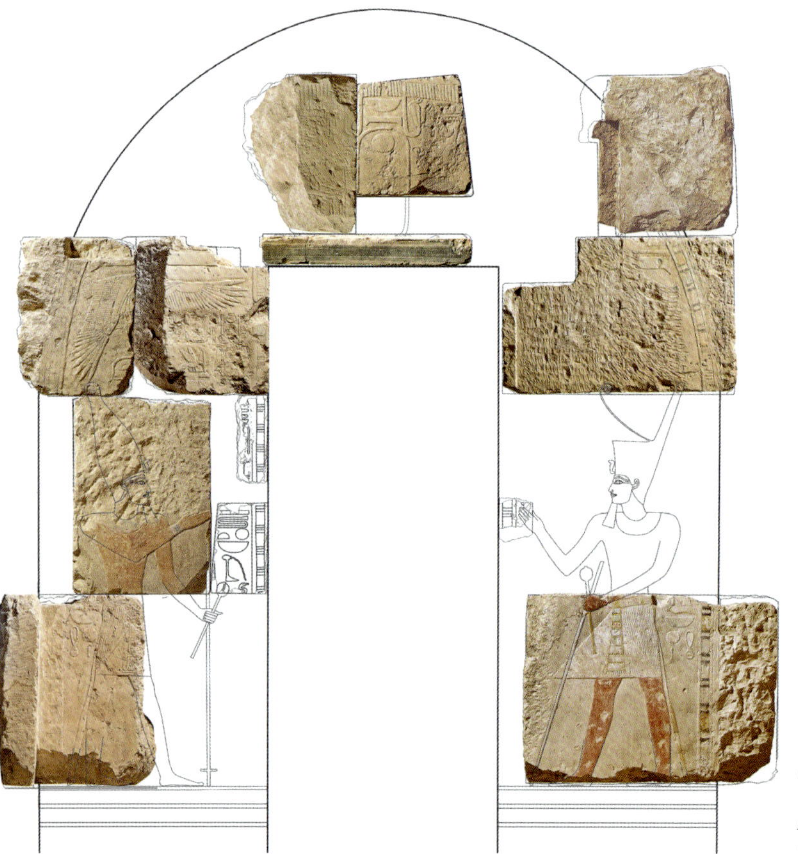

(Above) Partly preserved tympanum of the East wall of the Bark Hall prior to the restoration works. A representation of Horus Behdeti in the form of a winged sun disk is still visible below the embrasure of the ruined skylight situated in the outer wall of the main Sanctuary of Amun-Re.

(Left) Drawn reconstruction of the original entrance leading to the innermost chamber, where a cult statue was kept. Blocks inserted into the drawing have been found during the restoration works carried out by the Polish-Egyptian Mission in the Sanctuary. Both the theme and composition duplicate the decoration carved on the granite portal shown on the page 3. The wall was dismantled in the Ptolemaic period during the rearrangement of the Sanctuary.

(Above left)
Teresa Dziedzic studying the structure of the skylight. The interlocking blocks of the walls and the vault indicated that the skylight was executed together with the ceiling of the Bark Hall. In the reign of Hatshepsut the skylight was blocked, then reduced and reopened again. All changes were connected undoubtedly with the illumination of the statue kept in the innermost chamber of the Sanctuary.
(Above right)
The narrow and oblong aperture of the second skylight hewn out directly under the vault in the eastern wall of the Statue Room.
(Beside)
View of the undecorated interior of the skylight hewn out in the western wall of the Bark Hall. There are visible changes of its geometry and sloping threshold.

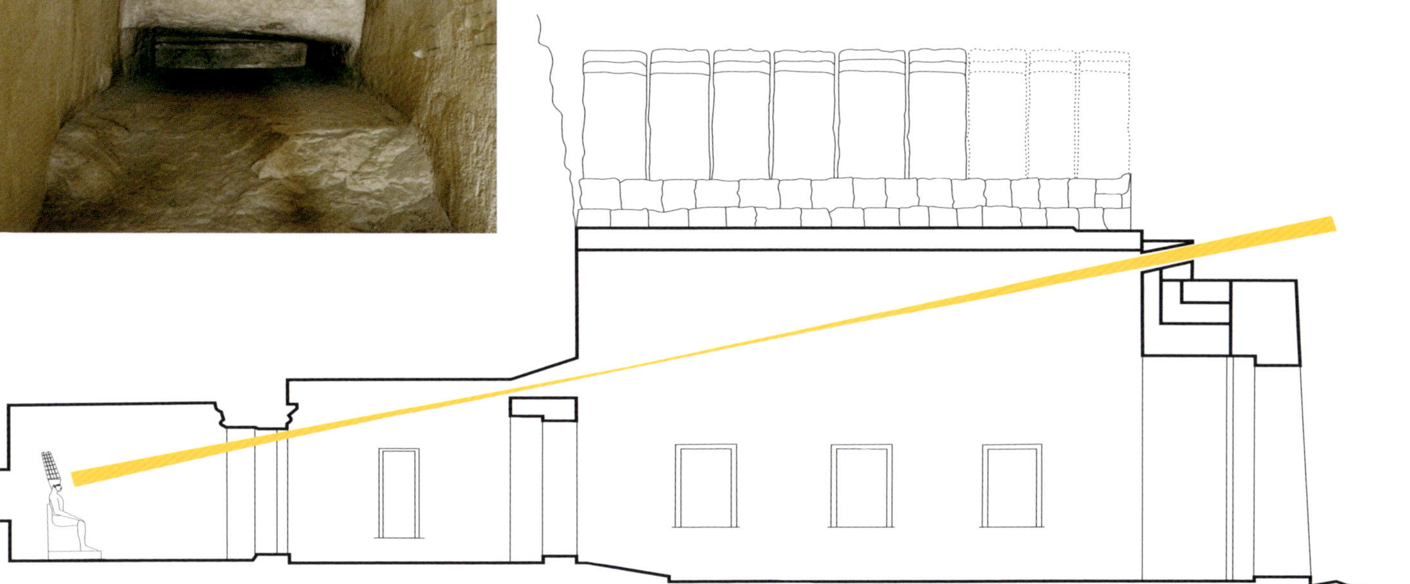

Cross-section of the Sanctuary. A luminous flux was precisely directed through the system of skylights hewn out in the walls of the Bark Hall and of the Statue Room into the innermost chamber. It is worth noting that a three day feast of Amun presumably fell on the days of the second month of Peret when sunlight penetrated into the Inner Sanctuary. The exact position of the cultic statue and its dimensions are theoretically calculated.

PROTECTION AND CONSERVATION PRIORITIES

The priority of the conservation activity of the Polish-Egyptian Mission is the preservation of the original substance of the Sanctuary, its stone structure as well as its polychrome, plasters and mortars. The exposed and unprotected tringle-shaped stone construction (photo below: the construction during conservation work), diverting sidewards the pressure above the corbelled vault of the Bark Hall, required the immediate intervention. As the result of a great and successful engineering project the original construction was protected. The façade wall and the protecting platform above the Upper Terrace were reconstructed. Pressure of stones and mountain rocks on the roof of the Sanctuary, as well as water penetration, were eliminated; the Sanctuary and the Upper Terrace are protected against rock fall (see photos on the next page from the left). In the Bark Hall, ancient deformations in the surface walls and the granite portal were stabilized. In the Hall, two of the four formerly existing statues of Hatshepsut in the form of the god Osiris were reconstructed; the walls were restored with many newly discovered, original decorated blocks (see photos on the next page, middle: Bark Hall before and after conservation work).

Continuous protecting works were conducted during the process of exchange of former stone blocks by newly discovered original decorated wall blocks. All the original blocks underwent full conservation treatment before montage, this means conservation of the paint, plaster and the stone itself. Preliminary conservation treatment consisted of reinforcement of paint layers, consolidation of pigments, ancient plasters and mortars. The layer of polychrome protected in this way underwent cleaning from thick layers of soot and dirt. The reliefs in the Sanctuary recovered their original intensive colours as a result of this treatment; it is visible in the representation of Tuthmosis III depicted in the west wall tympanum of the Bark Hall (see photos on the next page, right). A consequence of this work was identification of previously illegible graffiti, among others, cartouches with names of Hatshepsut and Horemheb or Greek graffiti from the Roman period. Attribution of colours to the royal representations in the Sanctuary or repainting of the Hatshepsut's representations in the Room of Cult Statue are consecutive effects of the conservation works.

PROTECTION AND CONSERVATION PRIORITIES

(Above to the left)
The representation of Hatshepsut's parents on the South wall of the Bark Hall: before and after conservation. Drawing of the missing head of queen Ahmes presented on page 21.
(Right) The representation of Tuthmosis III on the North wall of the Room of Cult Statue: before and after conservation.
(Below)
The final stage of the conservation work was an aesthetical treatment of fresh plasters and reconstruction of unpreserved outlines of figures in high relief. In this way, the contours of the two figures of the god of the Nile was marked in the ritual scene of sema-tawy on the northern wall of the Bark Hall, the scene was partly restored with the application of original fragments; in the same way, the outlines of the representation of a part of the holy bark of Amun, depicted on the opposite wall, was marked. To the left: Rajmund Gazda and Maria Lulkiewicz, two Polish conservators who conducted works in the Sanctuary.

كان نظام الإنارة معروفاً في العمارة الجنائزية في عصري الدولة القديمة والوسطى، لكن المعماري في حالتنا هذه كان مجبراً على تحديد مكانٍ لكُوَّتَيْن والربط بينهما وبين الوجهة الفلكية للمعبد بحيث تسقط أشعة الشمس في موعد محدد دقيق، على نقطة محددة، وليس من شك أن هذه النقطة كانت التمثال، أو وجهه الموجود في عمق المصلّى الأخير. ونلاحظ في الكُوَّتين آثار أعمال وتغييرات في القياسات، نُفذت في عهد حتشبسوت. وقد تأكّد أن أشعة الشمس__ في أثناء حكم الملكة حتشبسوت- كانت تدخل من خلال الكوّتين في: 15-25 من شهر نوفمبر وكذلك بين 12 و 22 من شهر فبراير وفي كلا الحالتين كانت الشمس تدخل صباحاً عند شروق الشمس.

في المرحلة الانتقالية الثالثة (1069-664 ق.م) كانت حجرات المعبد وغيرها من من المُصلّيات الموجودة في الشرفة العليا، تُستخدم لدفن أعضاء العائلات الملكية والوجهاء والكهنة. وكانت الوظائف العبادية للاحتفالات المرتبطة بطقوس " عيد الوادي" قد عادت إلى الدير البحري لفترة قصيرة في الفترة التي كان فيها "مينتو ايمحات" والياً على طيبة في منتصف القرن السابع قبل الميلاد. وكان المعبد الذي ردّم بفعل الهزّات الأرضية، قد طرأت عليه تغييرات أساسية، في عصر البطالمة في عهد بطليموس الثامن في النصف الأول من القرن الثاني قبل الميلاد، فقد شُيّد رواق أمام الواجهة بُنِيَ من عناصر متبقيّة من صفّ الأعمدة المتهدم في الشرفة العليا. وتحوَّلت الحجرة الأخيرة والتي كان فيها تمثال آمون رع المعبود يوماً إلى مصلّى لعبادة أَمْنحُتِب ابن حابو وإمْحُتِبْ، أما في المرحلة البيزنطيّة، فقد أُلحق قدس الأقداس بدير القديس "أبو فام" الذي كان قائماً منذ نهاية القرن السابع الميلادي في الشرفة العليا.

قدس الأقداس هو ما عليه اليوم بفضل أعمال البعثة البولندية المصرية لأعمال الآثار و الترميم التي ما تزال مستمرة منذ نصف قرن. منذ بداية أعمالنا كنا قد وضعنا نصب أعيننا أن نحافظ على المادة الأصليّة لهذا المعبد سواء كان على بنيته الحجرية أو ألوانه وكذلك الملاط أو طبقات الجصّ. وجاء النجاح في تنفيذ المشروع الهندسيّ- المعماريّ الذي شمل الحفاظ على سقف مقصورة المركب وبناء جدار ساتر مع رفّ صخري ليضمن الحماية لكل المبنى. كما توصّلنا إلى الصورة التي كان عليها العنصر الأخير من عناصر واجهة الشرفة. وقد اقتصرت أعمال الترميم والصيانة الأوليّة، على لصق وتفكيك طبقات اللوحات الجداريّة، وكذلك على تجميع الصبغيّات والطبقات الجصية والملاط المسحونة القديمة. وعلى هذه الشاكلة تخضع الطبقة المُلوّنة المصانة لعمليات تنظيف من الطبقات السميكة المترسّبة من السخام والأوساخ. وكانت النتيجة أنِ استردّت المنحوتاتُ النافرة ألوانها الأصليّة المُشرقة. وقد أغنت القطع الجداريّة الأصليّة التي عُثر عليها الديكورَ في مقصورة المركب. وكان لاكتشاف مشكاتَيْنِ وُسطيَّتين ،كانتا قد سُدَّتا في عصر البطالمة أهمية بالغة للغاية في تحديد الشكل المعماريّ النهائي للمعبد، وهذا بدوره سمح لنا بالوصول إلى صورة كاملة لدورة الطقوس التي كانت تُقام للعبادة اليومية وتقديم القرابين والهبات. وقد سمحت لنا الأجزاء من القطع الحجرية التي استخدمها البطالمة في سدّ هاتين المشكاتين سمحت باسترجاع صورة الزخرفة الجدارية في أسفل صورة المركب المقدس لآمون-رع. كما أن وضْع لوحة ترمز إلى مصر العليا ومصر السفلى سيماتاوي، تؤكّد على الدور الذي نُسب للمركب، والذي يوحد رمزيّاً بين بلدين هما مصر العليا ومصر السفلى وبين عالمين: عالم الأحياء وعالم الأموات، كما يؤكّد على مكانة آمون كإله لعرش البلدين الواقف على رأس الآلهة.

ترجمة: جورج يعقوب

مراجعة: محمود الطيب

ثديها المكشوف يفضح جنسها. ويتبدّل غطاء الرأس حسب الطقس أو مكان الصورة فتظهر بتاج أوزيريس أتف مزيّنٍ بقَرْنَيْ كبش أو بتاج أزرق خبريش، أو بالتاج الأحمر لمصر السفلى دشرت أو بشالات نمس أو شات. في السنة الثانية والأربعين لحكم تحتمس الثالث حوالي سنة 1437 ق.م. تم إزالة أسماء الملكة، المؤسِّسة وشوّهت صورها، ومما يلفت الانتباه أن التّلف طال بشكل خاص الردهة ومقصورة المركب، وفي نفس الوقت بقيت أغلب صور حتشبسوت في عمق المعبد على حالها دون أن تُمسّ. بالنسبة للرسومات الموجودة في مقصورة التمثال وبعد تنظيفها وإزالة طبقة السخام من فوقها أصبحت شاهداً على بدايات التغييرات اللونيّة في اللوحات التي تمثّل حتشبسوت والتي أجرتها الملكة نفسها. ولم يكن بالإمكان معرفة التغييرات في إيديولوجية عبادة الملكة لولا أعمال مُرمِّميّ البعثة البولندية-المصرية.

من خلال النعوت المرتبطة بآمون-رع (رُمِّمَت بعد عصر العمارنة) يمكننا القول إنّ طقوس العبادة كانت تُقام لِشَكلَيْن من أشكال تجسُّد آمون-رع: تجسُّد محلي في الدير البحري، وتجسّد آمون-رع القادم من الكرنك. وكانت طقوس العبادة اليومية تصوّر في نفس الوقت، وقائع طقس "فتح الفم" الذي كان يهدف إلى إحياء التمثال. وكانت طقوس العبادة هذه تقام على الأغلب أمام تماثيل، وُضعت في زوايا الحجرة الأولى لحتشبسوت، لكي تحمي المركب المقدس، وهي على شكل الإله أوزيريس حامي العالم الآخر. وكانت الملكة وبقية أعضاء الأسرة الملكية تستفيد من طقوس عبادة المذبح، والتي نجد صورها على جدران كل مشكاة. ومن المؤكّد أنّ طقس تقديم القربان كان مرتبطاً بعبادة الأسلاف التي كانت تشكّل بعداً هامّاً في الإيديولوجية الملكية، خاصّة وأنه على الرغم من أنّ المعبد كان مخصصاً لعبادة آمون- رع ، ومركبه المقدس، إلا أنه كان جزء من المعبد المخصص للعبادة الجنائزية، للملكة حتشبسوت. هنا تركّزت كلّ الأبعاد الإيديولوجية الملكية للملكة حتشبسوت، بما فيها علاقتها بوالدها المؤلَّه آمون. والدليل القاطع على ذلك أنّه قد أُضيف نعت خنمت آمون "المتحدة مع آمون" إلى اسمها حين ولادتها (الأولى بين السيدات النبيلات- حتشبسوت) .

ومعلوماتنا اليوم عن نظام ونشاط المعبد هي أفضل بما لا يُقاس عمّا كانت عليه من قبل وذلك بفضل دراسات النقوش والدراسات الآثارية التي تجريها البعثة البولندية- المصرية للآثار و الترميم . فقد ساعدت اللقى التي عُثر عليها أثناء أعمال الترميم على الوصول إلى تصوّر عن كيفيّة نشاطِ وعملِ الحجرة الأخيرة في المعبد. فقد كان الجميع يعتقد أنها كانت مُصلّى إضافيّاً نُحت في الصخر في عهد البطالسة، في الوقت الذي ثبت أنها كانت أهم حجرة في المحراب بل في المعبد كلّه. وقد صمّمت وبُنيت أثناء حكم الملكة حتشبسوت. فقد كان تمثال آمون-رع موجوداً هنا منذ البداية والذي كان يُضاء بنظام الكوّات.

على متن المركب في وسطه قدس الأقداس لتمثال الإله المعبود مذهّب ومُرصّع وقد حجبته مظلّة، لكننا لسنا متأكدين من أنّه كان موجوداً دائماً في خيمته. في الميمنة كانت تقليدياً توضع صورة تمثّل الإله معات وحتحتور والرايات الملكية وعليها أبو الهول بأشكال مختلفة.

اللوحات في المعبد، في الدير البحري تواكب بشكل جيد التغييرات التي طرأت على هيئة وشكل المركب المقدّس. في مرحلة الترميم بعد التخريب الذي حدث في فترة العَمارنة تم تكبير الصورة بشكل ملحوظ فقد أُضيفت للكباش تيجان أتف الفخمة عليها قرص الشمس ودروع أجويس. في وسط الدرع زخارف نباتية غنية تظهر الجعران– رمز الشمس المشرقة.

يزيّن سطح وأرضية المُصلّى إفريز يحتوي على كتابة مُشفَّرة لاسم حور محب الذي كان الحاكم الثاني الذي رمّم المنحوتات البارزة في المحراب بعد توت عنخ آمون. ويشارك في حفل تقديم القرابين أمام المركب: الملك وحرمه، حتشبسوت وربيبها تحتمس الثالث، وإبنتها الأميرة نفرو رع. وكان الحفل يتم بحضور الأموات من العائلة الملكية: تحتمس الأول، وأحمس والديّ حتشبسوت، وكذلك زوجها تحتمس الثاني، إضافة لأختها الأميرة نيفرو بيتي التي توفيت وهي في عمر الطفولة. ونلاحظ أنّ هؤلاء الذين يقيمون في العالم الآخر قد تجمّعوا في الجانب الغربي من الحجرة. وكانت الطقوس تستمرّ طوال الليل وتنتهي عند الفجر حين يبدأون بإطفاء المشاعل في أربع أحواض من الحليب. وقد تكون الأواني الموجودة حول القاعدة التي تحمل المركب ترمز إلى البحيرة التي كان المركب يبحر فيها.

الحدائق والخسّ والحقول المصوّرة على الشريط السفلي للزخرفة الجدارية، في مقصورة المركب تمثّل المجالات التي يشرف عليها ملك الآلهة آمون–رع في الكرنك. وعلى الأغلب كانت مثل هذه المواضيع تزين القاعدة المندثرة للمركب.

كان موكب العيد مع المركب يخرج مرّة في السنة، ولكنْ في نفس الوقت كانت تُمارس طقوس "العبادة اليومية" أمام التمثال المعبود في المعبد. وكان تمثاله يصوّر أروع شكل من أشكال حضور الإله في المعبد. ونجد أوصافاً لبعض عمليات العناية بالتمثال المعبود وطقوس تقديم القرابين في الأناشيد المكتوبة على جدران الرّدهة، كما صُوِّرت بعض وقائع الطقوس في ستّ مَشَاكٍ في مقصورة المركب المقدس. وتظهر الملكة في المشاكي برفقة أسلافها على عرش مصر، ومع وصيّ العرش — الشريك تحتمس الثالث، الذي يرافق حتشبسوت في كلّ الطقوس التي تُقام في المعبد.

هناك قاعدة سائدة مفادها أنّ الملكة فقط كانت الكاهن الأكبر في المشاكي، وفي أعلى أهم الجدران، والهياكل المتعارضة، حيث تمارس حتشبسوت الطقوس أمام تمثال الإله آمون–رع وقد إرتدت ثياباً ملكية رجالية، لكن

يجلبون الحيوانات المعدّة للذبح ثمّ يوزعون لحومها، بعد تقديمها كقرابين للإله، على المشاركين في الموكب. وكان مركب آمون يُوضع في قارب خاص أوسرحات، على الشاطىء وتجرُّه سفينة ملكية. على الضفة الغربية كان الموكب يتوقّف أمام معبد حتشبسوت السفلي أولاً، وغالباً ما كان يمرُّ على معبد تحتمس الأول خنمت–عنخ القريب، وبعدها يسير في طريق المواكب المشجّر نحو "مقصورة المركب" المَبنيّة قريباً من مبنى الشرفات في الدير البحري. هناك كانت تُقام طقوس الطهارة لتمثال الإله. وكانت الشعائر تصل إلى قمتها في " الباحة العليا" أما الختام فكان يتمّ في المحراب الرئيسيّ للمعبد، حيث كان مركب آمون المقدسُ وتمثال الإله المعبود يبيتان الليل هناك. ولذلك بُنيت الحجرة الأولى على شكل مستطيل، بحيث يمكن إقامة طقوس الأضاحي بسهولة مع وجود المركب في وسط الحجرة.

وتُزيّن هذه الطقوس جداريّ مقصورة المركب الطويلين بالكامل تقريباً. ونحن لا نرى القرابين مُشخّصة وقد تكدّست على الموائد والطاولات والحصائر فحسب، بل نجدها على هيئة مُجدْوَلة. فقد رُتّب فوق صورة المركب وفي صفّين 40 سجّلاً، تُشكّل قائمة القرابين مع كتابة باسم المنتوجات، وعددها بالكتابة التصويرية.

أكثر المنتوجات المعروضة في النحت البارز الملوّن هي قرابين تقليدية تُقدّم عادةً في طقوس المذبح والعبادات اليومية، فنجد أنواعاً من الخبز، وأشكالاً متنوعة من الحلويات إضافةً إلى البقوليات والخضروات، ومن بينها الخسّ والخِيار والبصل والثوم والكُرّاث، ونرى الفواكه ومن بينها التين والتمْر والعنب والرمّان، ونجد الدواجن من الإوزّ والبطّ، كما نجد وجبات من اللحم المشويّ، وفخذ العجل. وهناك وفْرة في المشروبات من بينها: مختلف أنواع البيرة والنبيذ والعسل والمياه العذبة، في أوعية مختلفة. ومما يلفت النظر،كميات الخسّ وباقات من الزهور التي كانت ترمز تقليدياً إلى الحياة والولادة، لأنهم كانوا يؤمنون أنها مليئة برائحة الإله.

ظلّت طريقة عبادة مركب آمون–رع المحمول من قبل الكهنة أثناء المواكب الاحتفالية على حالها دون تغيير عَبْر مئات السنين. لكنَّ المواضيع الزخرفيّة ازدادت وكبُر حجمها وازداد معها عدد الكهنة الذين يحملون المركب.

منذ البداية كان المركب الخشبي المطعّم بالذهب نموذجاً مُصغّراً لمركب النقلِ النهري، والذي كانت مقدمته ومؤخرته تُزيَّن بصورة لرأس الكبش وهو الحيوان المقدس لآمون. هكذا تبدو أقدم صور لمركب آمون المقدس على الجدران الكالستية للمقصورة التي بناها أمنحتب الأول في المعبد في الكرنك حوالي 1515– 1495 ق.م. وهكذا كان منظر المركب الأصلي في المحراب في معبد حتشبسوت في الدير البحري.

قدس الأقداس الرئيسي لآمون–رع

فرانتشيشك باڤليتسكي

لا بدّ أنّ قدس أقداس آمون–رع كان مُتفرِّداً وفخماً لدرجة أن معبد حتشبسوت الجنائزي كان يحمل اسم " بيت الإله العظيم آمون لملايين السنين. جسر جسرو". وكانت الملكة حتشبسوت قد شرعت في بنائه بُعيد تتويجها حوالي 1473 ق.م. وقد شُيّد قدس الأقداس في وسط الشرفة العليا أمام فناء مُعمَّد رحْب، يشكّل جداره الغربي واجهةً لقدس الأقداس. و يؤدّي مدخله المتموضع في الوسط عَبْر فناء مهيب إلى "مقصورة المركب" التي بُنيت في منحدر الكتلة الصخرية العالية. وقد نُحتَ في الصخر وعلى نفس المحور تماماً حجرتان: مقصورة التمثال المقدس ومعبد أو مُصلّى. وبفضل الدراسات العلمية التي أجرتها " البعثة البولندية– المصرية للآثار و الترميم"، توصلنا إلى تحديد الشكل والوظيفة الدينيّة لهاتين الحجرتين– والتي تعدُّ قضية أساسية لفهم كيفيّة نشاط وإدارة المعبد. في الحجرة الأخيرة يوجد *"قدس الأقداس، جسر جسرو"* *ويوجد* تمثال للإله الذي تُقدَّم له فروض العبادة بشكل يومي، وقد نُحت في الصخر مُصليّان جانبيان لعبادة التاسوع المقدس وعلى رأسه آمون–رع.

وفقاً لنظام العمارة في المعابد المصرية فإن الحجرة التالية تكون أصغر وأكثر انخفاضاً من الحجرة التي تليها وهكذا. وجاء اختيار المكان في نقطة إغلاق المحور الرئيسي للمعبد وفي أبعد وأعلى نقطة إلى الغرب في هذا المبنى ذي الشرفات، جاء هذا الاختيار ليضمن للإله الحميميّة الضروريّة. قبل المعبد وعلى امتداد هذا المحور فُتح شارع مُشجّر عريض للمواكب.وفي الجهة المقابلة من النيل تماماً شُيِّدت مجموعة معابد الكرنك، حيث كان موكب آمون —رع ينطلق مع مركبه نحو الدير البحري. وكان معبد آمون–رع على نفس النمط المعماري، رغم خراب وترميم لوحاته الجدارية والتماثيل التي كانت تزيّنه أكثر من مرّة، كان معبد آمون–رع هذا، يقوم بوظيفة مستودع رائع للمركب المقدس، والتمثال المعبود، وذلك حتى نهاية الدولة الحديثة. أمّا الطقوس الاحتفاليّة المتعلّقة بعبادة الملكة المؤسِّسة، فقد توقفت مع موتها حوالي 1458 ق.م.

في الفترة التي حكمت فيها الملكة كان المعبد في الكرنك مكاناً يُبحر منه موكب العيد ومعه التمثال ومركب آمون–رع المقدسُ في الشهر الصيفيّ الثاني شمو. كان الموكب الكبير، يخرج بمشاركة الحاكم مع فرقة عسكرية، والوجهاء والكهنة، من الكرنك نحو النيل حاملاً تمثال الإله في قدس الأقداس، على ظهر مركب المواكب. وكانوا إضافةً لذلك يحملون رايات الآلهة والرايات الملكية وتماثيل الحكّام والأواني الطقوسيّة وكمّاً هائلاً من القرابين. وكانوا

SELECTED READING

Barwik, M. (2010). Sanctuary of the Hatshepsut temple at Deir el-Bahari. In M. Dolińska and H. Beinlich (eds), *8. Ägyptologische Tempeltagung: Interconnections between temples; Warschau, 22.–25. September 2008* (pp. 1–12). Wiesbaden

Barwik, M. (2016). A record of offerings from the Temple of Hatshepsut in Deir el-Bahari: ostrakon DeB Inv. No. 85/75. In A. Łajtar, A. Obłuski, and I. Zych (eds), *Aegyptus et Nubia christiana. The Włodzimierz Godlewski jubilee volume on the occasion of his 70th birthday* (pp. 665–677). Warsaw

Bauer, K. and Krzyżanowski, L. (eds). (1979). *The temple of Queen Hatshepsut* I–IV. Warsaw

Ćwiek, A. (2007). Red, yellow and pink: ideology of skin hues at Deir el-Bahari. *Fontes Archaeologici Posnanienses*, 43, 23–50

Dodson, A. (1988). Two royal reliefs from the temple of Deir el-Bahari. *The Journal of Egyptian Archaeology*, 74, 212–214

Godlewski, W. (1986). *Le monastère de St Phoibammon* [=*Deir el-Bahari* 5]. Warsaw

Iwaszczuk, J. (2011). The names of the doors and domains in the Temple of Hatshepsut at Deir el-Bahari. Question of erasures of the feminine endings. *Études et Travaux*, 24, 109–115

Karkowski, J. (1992). Notes on the Beautiful Feast of the Valley as represented in Hatshepsut's Temple at Deir el-Bahari. In S. Jakobielski and J. Karkowski (eds), *50 years of Polish excavations in Egypt and the Near East: Acts of the Symposium at the Warsaw University 1986* (pp. 155–166). Warsaw

Karkowski, J., Winnicki, J.K., and Brecciani, E. (1983). Amenhotep, son of Hapu and Imhotep at Deir el-Bahari: some reconsiderations. *Mitteilungen des Deutschen Archäologischen Instituts. Abteilung Kairo*, 39, 93–105

Kitchen, K.A. (1963). A long-lost portrait of princess Neferurē from Deir el-Baḥri. *The Journal of Egyptian Archaeology*, 49, 38–40

Laskowska-Kusztal, E. (1984). *Le sanctuaire ptolémaïque de Deir el-Bahari* [=*Deir el-Bahari* 3]. Warsaw

Łajtar, A. (2006). *Deir el-Bahari in the Hellenistic and Roman periods: A study of an Egyptian temple based on Greek sources* [=*The Journal of Juristic Papyrology Supplement* 4]. Warsaw

Marciniak, M. (1978). Un reçu d'offrande de Deir el-Bahari. *Bulletin de l'Institut Français d'Archéologie Orientale*, 78, 165–170

Naville, E. (1906). *The temple of Deir el Bahari* V. *The Upper Court and Sanctuary* [=*Memoir of the Egypt Exploration Fund* 27]. London

Pawlicki, F. (2007). Princess Neferure in the Temple of Queen Hatshepsut at Deir el-Bahari. Failed heiress to the Pharaoh's throne? *Études et Travaux*, 21, 109–127

Pawlicki, F. (2016). Four seasons of documentation in the Main Sanctuary of Amun-Re in the Temple of Hatshepsut at Deir el-Bahari. *Polish Archaeology in the Mediterranean*, 25, 303–314

Roehrig, C., Dreyfus, R., and Keller, C.A. (eds). (2005). *Hatshepsut: From Queen to Pharaoh*. New York

Sankiewicz, M. (2015). The iconography of co-rule at Deir el-Bahari: Hatshepsut and Tuthmosis III in the Statue Room of the Main Sanctuary of Amun. In Z.E. Szafrański (ed.), *Deir el-Bahari studies* [=*Polish Archaeology in the Mediterranean* 24/2] (pp. 161–168). Warsaw

Schott, S. (1937). Das Löschen von Fackeln in Milch. *Zeitschrift für Ägyptische Sprache und Altertumskunde*, 73, 1–25

Szafrański, Z.E. (ed.). (2001). *Królowa Hatszepsut i jej świątynia 3500 lat później = Queen Hatshepsut and her temple 3500 years later*. Warsaw

Szafrański, Z.E. (2007). King (?) Neferure, daughter of kings Tuthmosis II and Hatshepsut. *Études et Travaux*, 21, 139–150

Winlock, H.E. (1942). *Excavations at Deir el Bahri, 1911–1931*. New York

Wysocki, Z. (1985). The discovery and reintegration of two niches in the East Chamber of the Queen Hatshepsut's Main Sanctuary at Deir el-Bahri. In P. Posener-Kriéger (ed.), *Mélanges Gamal Eddin Mokhtar* II [=*Bibliothèque d'Étude* 97/2] (pp. 361–378). Cairo